Vanessa Bates is an award-winning playwright for stage and radio and also writes for film and television. She has been an affiliate playwright of the Sydney Theatre Company and Griffin Theatre with plays also produced by Malthouse, Deckchair and Vitalstatistix Theatre. Her work has won the NSW Premier's Literary Award and been shortlisted for the Victorian Premier's Literary Award, the Patrick White Playwright Award and the Griffin Award.

Angie Diaz as Jane and Jackson Vaughan as Jed in Tantrum Youth Arts' 2016 production. (Photo: Claire Albrecht)

TRAILER

VANESSA BATES

Currency Press, Sydney

CURRENCY PLAYS

First published in 2018
by Currency Press Pty Ltd,
PO Box 2287, Strawberry Hills, NSW, 2012, Australia
enquiries@currency.com.au
www.currency.com.au

Typeset by Dean Nottle for Currency Press.
Cover design by Lisa White for Currency Press.

Currency Press acknowledges the Traditional Owners of the Country on which we live and work. We pay our respects to all Aboriginal and Torres Strait Islander Elders, past and present.

Contents

Tallulah Cobbin as Keera and Jackson Vaughan as Jed in Tantrum Youth Arts' 2016 production. (Photo: Claire Albrecht)

INTRODUCTION

Being isolated in a perceived dead-end town is a feeling relatable to many teenagers. I experienced it myself, as a young girl growing up in the Hunter Region of NSW. I struggled with the conflict of feeling compelled to escape yet bound to stay, tempted by the comforts of familiar territory, home and family. It was only after I moved away that I gained perspective and could see that the place in which I grew up really wasn't that bad, and that many things I had earlier deemed insignificant had become unique and even special. I began to value my childhood experiences, sheltered from the bright lights and busy pace of the city. The disaffection transformed to affection. It is the complexity of relationship to place, negotiated during a journey of self-discovery, that lies at the heart of *Trailer*.

Tantrum Youth Arts commissioned Vanessa Bates to write a play giving voice to young people and regional stories in Wyong, NSW. With the support of Wyong Shire Council and Arts NSW, Tantrum facilitated workshops with young people living on the NSW Central Coast, with Bates and local theatre director Anna Kerrigan. What they uncovered in these workshops were a variety of subjects: isolation; being caught between two worlds; home vs. unfamiliar territories; fractured and single-parent families; the railway; unemployment; social media; rumours and fame; identity and loss. All of these informed the creation of *Trailer*.

Bates paints the Central Coast and Wyong as unprogressive and conservative; as in-between places, destinations on a train line connecting two cities: Sydney and Newcastle. This allows the audience to imagine that growing up with two mums may not have been an easy experience for Jed in his youth. The bluntness with which a fellow passenger dismisses *Dallas Buyers Club* through casual homophobia illuminates the idea that Jed is living in a place that has the potential to stymie his growth.

PASSENGER: I didn't like that one actually. Too long. Also. Too gay. (p.6)

The theme of isolation is introduced early in the play. The play opens on the train with each cast member wearing earphones, tuned into a device, not making contact or speaking out loud. The inherent irony in this setting is that as we view a group of people sharing a communal experience, it quickly dawns on the audience that each person exists in complete isolation from one another. We see disparate worlds coexist, as we hear snippets of podcasts and music revealing the differing tastes of the commuters. Following this arresting movement and sound sequence it becomes evident that nobody wants to disrupt this status quo, even when there is perceived danger threatening a fellow commuter. The real tension driving this scene, however, is in the friction between Jed's inner yearning to intervene and his frozen (passive) physical state.

> JED: And I think: I should have got up.
> I should have helped them.
> I should have saved them. (p.3, Scene One)

The opening's movement and soundscape sequence is repeated two times later throughout the play. This repetition serves to both depict the unwaveringly monotonous nature of the commute and to allow us to vicariously experience Jed's world.

Bates uses the train as a powerful metaphor. The train becomes life itself, a force that moves forward like time: you can sit back and observe or you can take charge, take action. For much of the play we see Jed as a passenger, both literally on the train and metaphorically in his own life. As he rides the train, physically transported from one place to another, it becomes increasingly clear that this is not due to his agency, but rather Jed has become the eponymous trailer, forever being pulled along, never at the wheel. In many instances we see both Jed and Keera ride the trains simply for fun, or use them as an escape, a place to sit, think, observe, or to run away. For Jed there is safety in the isolation of the quiet carriage and Bates uses syncopated rhythms in the dialogue to create the somnambulistic ambience in which Jed finds comfort.

Like Jed, other patrons largely keep to themselves on the train, earphones in, not talking, but Keera pulls Jed from his insular world by proclaiming the sight of him as an exciting celebrity spotting moment.

KEERA: [*loudly*] Your dad's a movie star!

JED: Don't—

KEERA: You're a little bit famous! (p.4)

We find out a rumour exists in Wyong that Jed is the lovechild of a famous Hollywood actor. This is not a trivial detail in Jed's life; in many ways, it has become forged with his very identity. Keera's assertion brings the carriage to life in a comical guessing game about who Jed's father is, elevating him from his perceived mundane existence in the process.

We come to understand that this rumour has been fundamental to Jed's sense of self-worth. Being associated with fame has made him feel special. It is evident that Jed didn't necessarily invest in the truth of this rumour, but nevertheless it has remained a crucial facet of his being. The confirmation of his suspicions about the veracity of this rumour in the latter half of the play therefore has an abruptly shattering effect, and marks a turning point in Jed's life.

JED: But having someone famous for a dad, even if I didn't
     actually have him …
     …
     I had the spark. Because of him. And now, it's gone…
     and I'm falling.
     …
     I'm just ordinary, Keera. I'm just like anyone else, made
     up from an ordinary egg and a very ordinary sperm.
     I'm sorry.
         Beat.
     I'm not playing anymore. (pp.26,34)

The fantasy is over and in this powerful declarative statement, we understand that it is time for Jed to confront the truth about his existence. The idealised intangible presence of his father dissolves and Jed begins to reckon with the corporeal devastation being experienced by Caryl, his birth mum, who has actually played a tangible role in his life. Towards the end of the play Frank helps Jed see that his 'spark' has nothing to do with his absent father, but that it comes from the strength and courage within.

FRANK: I'm not saying she'll get better, nothing like that.
Just that, I can tell, you'll get through this. You got a
spark in you. (p.37)

Jed finally takes action and visits his mother in hospital. He once again boards the train, but where there was previously isolation, there is now connection to a purpose; where there was somnambulance, Jed is now fiercely awake.

He has reached legal adulthood, but Jed will not achieve true maturation until he can fully define and understand himself. Jed's two mums Caryl and Jane had protected him by not telling him the truth: both in regards to Jed's father, and about the severity of Caryl's illness. Later we find out this was not a selfless act, but rather an act of self-preservation, as Jane is struggling to cope with the news. Jed describes the hole in his gut in language that evokes a carcinogenic tumour, his emotional torment paralleling Caryl's physical suffering.

JED: Sometimes it feels like I've got this hole here in my
gut, getting bigger and bigger every day. (p.37)

Bates uses the symbol of the sinkhole to give this impending loss an onstage presence. This is cleverly done, as Caryl's character never appears onstage. The physical presence of the sinkhole, in conjunction with Keera's fascination with it, is a reminder of just how fast and unexpectedly loss can occur. The ground can fall out from under us in a few moments.

KEERA: You see the second brother, crying, and you wonder
if he'll ever survive that grief. It's like a gap, a part of
him missing, left by someone who just disappears. (p.29)

Trailer explores vital issues of identity, family, self-discovery and loss. The story manages to be both intimate and universal in its appeal, as we follow a young man who realises what he needs to do in order to truly live, instead of simply existing. As many teenagers feel dissatisfaction with the place in which they grew up, they too feel that their own stories are uninteresting and not worthy of being shared, but this commission saw the immense value of the struggles and experiences of young people living in regional areas. Bates' mastery lies in uncovering the special things within people, especially when these people don't yet see it themselves.

Lucy Shepherd
Newcastle, 2018

Lucy Shepherd is a theatre maker, performer, director and arts educator. She is the Artistic Director of Tantrum Youth Arts, Newcastle, and a co-founder of contemporary performance collective, Paper Cut.

This play is for Tristan and for Christopher.

Trailer was first produced by Tantrum Youth Arts at The Art House, Wyong, NSW, on 12 May 2016, with the following cast:

KEERA	Tallulah Cobbin
JANE	Angie Diaz
FRANK / KEERA'S FATHER	Christopher Saunders
JED	Jackson Vaughan

All minor roles, including train passengers, were shared between the actors.

Director, Anna Kerrigan
Designer, Joshua Maxwell
Design Mentor, Tobhiyah Stone Feller
Lighting Designer, Lyndon Buckley
Sound Designer, Jess Blackburn
Producer, Tamara Gazzard

The original production of *Trailer* was supported by Arts NSW, Wyong Shire Council and The Art House; and developed with the support of Playwriting Australia in the National Script Workshop 2015.

Special thanks to Amy Hardingham, Stuart Slough, Tamara Gazzard, Lucy Shepherd, Claire Albrecht, Anna Kerrigan, Joshua Maxwell, Tim Roseman and Jane FitzGerald.

CHARACTERS

JED, 19. Grew up and went to school in Wyong on the Central Coast. All of his school friends have left and gone to jobs or uni in Sydney or Newcastle.

KEERA, mid teens. Sister of a girl who was in Jed's year at school.

JANE, 40s. Long-term partner of Caryl, Jed's mother.

FRANK, 40s. Works at the council. He is one of those people who seems abrupt on the outside but has a heart of gold.

PASSENGERS

RAILWAY ANNOUNCER

GUY ON TRAIN

KEERA'S FATHER

POLICE OFFICER

PISSED-OFF BLOKE

All the actors at times play another character, usually a passenger on the train. They may flip from one character to another within a line or two.

SETTING

Wyong, a town on the Central Coast of New South Wales. The train line through Wyong goes south to Sydney or north to Newcastle.

NOTE

Scenes One, Seven, Thirteen and Sixteen can be thought of as movement pieces/breathing spaces. These are on a carriage on a train. The last turns into a more naturalistic scene when Jane and Jed appear.

The train rhythm should put emphasis on the second syllable:

Ch *ch*, ch *ch*
ch *ch*, ch *ch* …

SCENE ONE

Sound of a train.

PASSENGERS *move onto the train space.*

Soundtrack starts.

Nobody makes contact. Nobody speaks out loud.

Everyone is wearing or looking at a device.

Everyone wears earphones.

Some people text.

Some people listen to music or are mid-conversation. Soundtrack is made of snippets of music, grunge or classical, podcasts or a recorded conversation.

This movement piece seamlessly moves into next scene.

Soundtrack fades into ...

Sound of the train.

SCENE TWO

Sound of the train continues.

RAILWAY ANNOUNCER: A reminder that there are three quiet carriages on this train. They are the first, last and central carriages. Passengers are asked to refrain from loud conversations, playing music or using your mobile phones in these carriages.

    JED *is on the train with other* PASSENGERS.

JED: I see this guy, he's wearing a cap ... one of those trucker caps, and sunglasses. Sort of asleep ...

ACTOR 4: Starts up, soon after we leave the station, saying something under his breath.

JED: First I can't even hear him, but soon I can just make out.

ACTOR 2: Noises.

    Words.

    Rhythmic.

    Goes with the sound of the train.

ACTOR 3: Ch *ch*, ch *ch*
ch *ch*, ch *ch* …

JED: But it's

GUY: Fuck *fuck*, fuck *fuck*
Fuck *fuck*, fuck *fuck* …

ACTOR 4: And—

JED: We're in the top of the quiet carriage, that's my preferred carriage: the quiet carriage

ACTOR 3: the quiet carriage, the one at the front, he's got his back to the engine,

JED: I'm a few seats back with my head down but watching, and I realise I can hear other voices,

ACTOR 2: further down, must be in the front bit of the carriage

JED: I can hear other voices, these two women. I think one's younger and one's older because of the way they talk to each other,

ACTOR 2: the younger one's really polite

ACTOR 3: and the older one's a bit of a know-it-all

ACTORS 2 & 3: [*together*] and they both talk *really* loudly.

JED: And I realise they haven't stopped talking since we left the station …

ACTOR 3: Sort of breathe out, exhalation,

ACTOR 2: avalanche of words …

OLDER WOMAN PASSENGER: My mother, your mother,

YOUNGER WOMAN PASSENGER: my family, your family,

OLDER WOMAN PASSENGER: his wedding, her wedding,

YOUNGER WOMAN PASSENGER: my father, your son.

JED: But now the guy in the cap, he's talking too, under the rhythm of the train

GUY: Fuck *fuck*, fuck *fuck*
Fuck *fuck*, fuck *FUCK!*

JED: He's getting angrier, and his voice is getting louder and

ACTOR 4: suddenly he sort of lurches up out of his seat and he's heading down the stairs towards the women

JED: and I think: I should get help

ACTOR 3: help them, get up

ACTOR 2: do something!

JED: Ch *ch*, ch *ch*
ch *ch*, ch *ch* …

ACTOR 4: They obviously can't see him or can't hear him and their voices are getting louder

JED: ch *ch*, ch *ch!*

ch *ch*, ch *ch!* ...

ACTOR 3: *You should*

ACTOR 2: *get out*

ACTOR 3: *have fun*

ACTOR 2: *you're young!*

GUY: *Fuck fuck, fuck fuck*

fuck fuck, fuck fuck!

JED: And then. That second where voices overlap, he must be right next to them,

ACTOR 4: he must be standing right over them,

JED: and I hear him yell:

GUY: It's really fucking noisy in here for a so-called quiet carriage!

Slight pause.

JED: And I think: I should have got up.

I should have helped them.

I should have saved them.

And then

I hear them say ...

Slight pause.

ACTOR 2: Shhhhhhhhhh.

JED: Like you say to a kid.

ACTOR 3: Shhhhhh.

ACTORS 2, 3 & 4: [*together*] Shhhhhhhhhhhh.

Slight pause.

JED: I think he might attack them. Or knife them. Or something.

Beat.

But he doesn't.

Pause.

RAILWAY ANNOUNCER: Next stop is Tuggerah. Tuggerah next stop.

JED: He gets out at the next stop.

ACTOR 4: Still muttering. Still swearing under his breath.

ACTOR 2: Watch him walk along the platform. The train picks up speed
JED: and then … he's gone.

Pause.

JED *is still watching out the window as* KEERA, *in school uniform,*
startles him.

KEERA: Hey! It's you!
JED: What …?
KEERA: I know you.
JED: No you don't.
PASSENGER 3: Shhhh.
KEERA: I do. You were in my sister's year.
PASSENGER 4: Excuse me. This is a quiet carriage.
JED: Sorry. Sorry about that. [*To* KEERA] This is a quiet carriage.
KEERA: [*loudly*] Your dad's a movie star!
JED: Don't—
KEERA: You're a little bit famous!

Other PASSENGERS *are looking.* JED *feels self-conscious.*

JED: Stop that.
KEERA: He lives in Hollywood. He won an Academy Award! [*To the*
train] He won an Oscar!
JED: Okay, stop it, alright.
KEERA: What was that movie he won the Oscar for?

Silence. JED *is torn.* PASSENGERS *are fascinated.*

Failure To Launch?
JED: [*horrified*] No.
KEERA: *How To Lose A Guy In 10 Days*? *The Wedding Planner*?
JED: No. Obviously.

Beat.

Those are … rom-coms.
PASSENGER 4: What about … oh, what's it called?
PASSENGER 3: *Magic Mike*?
PASSENGER 4: No … um … he was really good … what was it ?… It'll
come …
PASSENGER 3: *Wolf of Wall Street*?

PASSENGER 4: Come off it, he only had five scenes … No … it was sort of … science fiction.

JED: *Interstellar.*

PASSENGER 4: *Interstellar*! That's it. [*To* JED] He was very good in that.

KEERA: [*to* JED] Was *that* what he won the Oscar for?

JED: No.

He looks around, the carriage is waiting to hear.

Fine.

Slight pause.

Dallas Buyers Club.

PASSENGERS & KEERA: Yes! Of course! Knew it!

KEERA: He played the role of cowboy Ron Woodroof. The film earned wide critical acclaim and he won many acting awards, including the Golden Globe Award for Best Actor—Drama, and … the Academy Award for Best Actor in 2014!

PASSENGERS *applaud.*

PASSENGER 3: [*to* JED] So, you're saying … what … he's your father?

KEERA: Yes! He's a little bit famous, I said that. Didn't I, Jed? [*To* PASSENGERS] Look at his face.

PASSENGERS *look at* JED. *Can't really see the resemblance.*

JED: People say I look like my mum.

PASSENGER 4: Movie star on the Coast. I remember that. Years ago.

KEERA: He was an exchange student. Here for a year. Met a local girl. Went back to America, became a big movie star.

PASSENGER 3: [*to* JED] Must be nice for you. Been over to visit much?

JED: No.

KEERA: How great would it have been if you'd gone to the Oscars with him? Wouldn't that have been great?

Everyone looks at JED. *Excruciating.*

RAILWAY ANNOUNCER: Next stop is Wyong. Wyong next stop.

JED: That's me.

KEERA: Me too. Wait up!

Beat. They're gone.

PASSENGER 3: *Dallas Buyers Club.*

PASSENGER 4: I didn't like that one actually. Too long. Also. Too gay.

> *Sound of a train rattling past.*

SCENE THREE

Caryl, Jane and Jed's house.

JED *putting on his work clothes.*

He watches as JANE *rushes past with a suitcase.*

She rushes back. Flustered.

She rushes back the other way with a violin case and other items. She stops. Sniffs.

JANE: Are you wearing deodorant?

JED: Yes.

JANE: [*unconvinced*] Mmm.

> *She rushes past.* JED *takes the opportunity to quickly spray on some deodorant.*
>
> JANE *comes back. She's still carrying the violin case.*
>
> *He gives her a look.*

She wanted the violin. I said there's no point, they won't let you play in the hospital. FYI. You look great.

JED: LOL. Thanks. … Are you okay?

JANE: Yes … It's just. Seeing you in a tie. You look like … like someone with a proper job.

JED: That's because I am … someone with a proper job.

JANE: And you look so …

> *Almost teary.* JED *is embarrassed. She wants to take a photo on her phone.*

JED: Bloody hell, Jane, don't …

JANE: It's for Caryl.

> *She takes a pic.*

One more.

> *Another.*

Reminds me of your first day at school. I cried then too. **Remember?** Actually, Mum and I were both crying.

JED: Haven't you got a train to catch?

JANE: It's the eight thirty-three, I've got plenty of time. Sort of. I wish you were coming with me, alright? There, I've said it.

JED: You want me to miss my first day? First impressions count. You told me that.

JANE: I know, I know … To tell the truth, I thought tomorrow was your first day.

JED: No. Today. I mean, if you think I should come with you … But she said it was just tests. She said I shouldn't be worried.

Slight pause.

So is it? Just tests?

JANE: It is. Just tests. And she's right—you shouldn't be worried.

JED: And she'll be back soon anyway? Tomorrow? Next day?

JANE: Probably. I mean yes, you're right.

JED: So. I should go to work.

JANE: Yes. Caryl wants you to go to work. I want you to go to work. This is a good job, it could lead to … other good jobs. We all know how hard it is around here. Most of your friends had to go.

JED: All my friends.

JANE: Yes. And that's why … your two mums want you to go to work.

Beat.

And wear deodorant.

JED: Jane!

JANE: I know I know. Let me help fix your tie.

As she does.

JED: They'll give me all the shit jobs, won't they? 'Cause I'm new.

JANE: That's what newbies get to do.

JED: Play those lame jokes. Say things like … 'Go and ask for a left-handed spanner' or 'Go and ask for a long stand'.

JANE: Yeah. [*Laughing*] My dad used to do that too. On the old trains, there was this big wheel at the front which was actually the brake. They used to tell newbies to hold onto that wheel so they could steer the train. [*Laughing*] Hold onto that wheel.

JED *isn't laughing.* JANE *tries to explain.*

You can't steer a train. The tracks do.

She laughs. JED *doesn't.*

Okay, I better go. Good luck on your first day. First impressions. Important. Love you.

She pecks him on the cheek. Goes to leave, stops a moment.

I'll tell her ... you'll see her soon?

JED: Sure. Tell her to hurry up and come home.

JANE *nods and leaves. Violin case left on the table.*

SCENE FOUR

Office. JED *stands waiting as* FRANK *looks at his paperwork.*

FRANK: Yep.

Pause.

Yep.

Pause.

Yep.

Silence.

[*Finally*] Not bad.

JED: Sorry, what?

FRANK: Your exam results. Not bad.

JED: Thanks.

FRANK: Not good though, were they?

JED *shrugs.*

No, hang on, my mistake. Says here you did well in 'Art'.

More waiting. FRANK *is making little notes.*

Jed.

JED: Yes?

FRANK: With a J.

JED: That's right.

FRANK: Jed. Is that short for something? Jeremy? Jebediah?

JED: Just ... Jed.

Pause.

FRANK: Just ... Jed.

He makes a little note.

So you wanted to start a bit early? Twenty-four hours early. Don't want to start on the start date we sent you: tomorrow. You want to start today. Any reason for that? Dental appointment? Meant to have a tooth pulled, were you?

Slight pause. JED *searches for a reason.*

JED: No reason. I'm just ... keen. First impressions. All that.

FRANK: Keen. Keen as mustard.

JED: Yeah. Is that wrong?

FRANK: No. I like a kid with a bit of oomph, has a bit of ... what do you call it ...?

JED: Initiative?

FRANK: I call it really bloody annoying. You're meant to be doing training on the job. That starts tomorrow. But you don't want to start tomorrow. You want to start today. So now, you have to do something different. Something special.

Beat.

Alright, got something special here for you to check out.

JED: Great.

FRANK: Yep. This. [*Indicating a piece of paper*] It might be bull. Probably is bull. But we have to check these things out, don't we, Jeremy?

JED: Jed.

FRANK: Yep. People ring up about every damn thing. Up to us to show some interest, give some reassurance. 'Got a possum in my roof.' 'Got a bunyip in the creek.' This one says they've got a sinkhole in their yard.

JED: [*slightly alarmed*] A sinkhole? Are you sure that's a job you want me to do? This is my first day.

FRANK: Pfft. S'not a sinkhole. Mine subsidence possibly. Or more likely old sewer pipes, leaking underground. If it's in the road ... pothole, not sinkhole.

JED: [*still alarmed*] Mine subsidence? How am I meant to ...?

FRANK: Relax, Jeremy. Just quietly, we get calls from this place a lot.

JED: Why don't you fix it then?

FRANK: Because I told you, it's a load of bull. You just need to talk to them, have a look, let us know if there's anything, which there won't be. Geez, Jeremy, you look a bit uptight there, mate. Relax. Pretend you're in one of your dad's movies or something.

JED: [*startled*] Piss off.

FRANK: Much better. You kids today. You think you're special. You think you deserve special treatment, well you don't. Screw this up and you're back to Centrelink.

He hands over a piece of paper and a clipboard.

There you go.

Beat.

Reckon that's probably a long enough stand, don't you?

He laughs as JED *exits.*

SCENE FIVE

Keera's house. JED *on the porch.*

KEERA: [*from inside*] I'll get it! It's alright, I'll get it.

A moment. JED *looks at his clipboard. Nervous.* KEERA *comes outside. Happy to see him.*

Hello!

JED *looks at her.*

JED: [*realising*] Oh, great. You.

KEERA: We met on the train.

JED: Someone put you up to this? Was it Frank?

KEERA: On the quiet carriage …

JED: Frank from work? 'Cause that's just … just …

KEERA: What?

JED: This is my first day of work. It's alright for you, you're still at school. Everything's a laugh for you.

KEERA: That's not true. Everything's not a laugh for me.

Silence. Slight noise from the house. JED *looks up at the house.*

JED: Is someone there? In your house?

> KEERA *doesn't look around.*

KEERA: My dad.

> *Slight pause.*

Watching.

> *Silence.* JED *nods, looks at his clipboard. Nervous again.*

JED: Um … good morning. My name is Jed Bowden, I'm from the council. There was a call asking to check out this address, specifically a …

> *He looks at his clipboard.*

Hole.

KEERA: A *sink* hole.

JED: No. no. Probably *not* a sinkhole. Mine subsidence possibly. Or more likely old sewer pipes, leaking underground. If it's in the road … pothole, not sinkhole. Was it you that called?

KEERA: Was that wrong, am I underage for a sinkhole?

JED: No. Where is it? The … hole. Can you show me, Miss … um …

> *He shuffles his papers, looking.*

What's your name?

KEERA: Do you need a hint?

JED: No. It doesn't matter. Just show me the hole.

KEERA: Remember Suzanne? In Geography?

JED: Um. No.

KEERA: You had a big crush on her and you stole her pencil case.

JED: Ah, no, to both those things.

KEERA: It's alright. She hated that pencil case anyway. Plus she said: you were really cute with the crush thing. Your face used to go red whenever she said something to you. Yeah, like that. I'm Keera. Her sister. And you're Jed. And I know all about you.

JED: [*slightly alarmed*] No you don't.

> *Slight pause.* KEERA *glances up at the window.*

KEERA: [*to* JED] So, you want to see the um …

JED: Hole.

KEERA: Sinkhole?

JED: Purported … sinkhole yes. Please.
KEERA: There.

She shows him a very small hole in the ground. Very unimpressive.

JED: Is that it?
KEERA: Yes.
JED: You think that's a … sinkhole. Why exactly do/you—?
KEERA: It's gotten bigger. That's what sinkholes do. They get bigger.
JED: Right. But usually, pretty fast.
KEERA: This is a slow one. Are you going to measure it?

He takes his pen and pushes it at the hole.

You should measure it properly. You shouldn't just … poke it.
JED: Why? Because the lid might fall off my pen?
KEERA: No. Because you might start it crumbling.
JED: Crumbling?
KEERA: Crumbling and getting bigger and swallowing the yard and the house and the cars. There are sinkholes that have swallowed up building blocks.
JED: But not in Wyong.
KEERA: In America. And various other countries. Like China. You should thank me for letting you know. The council should thank me.

Pause.

JED: Sure.

He looks at her carefully.

I'm going to … measure this properly, okay? You should probably stand back.

He begins to measure it. She backs away.

KEERA: Sue's in Sydney now. I really miss her. Her friend Katy moved there too. She lives in Newtown. She's only been there a month and she's got a nose-ring and tattoos all up her arm. Her mum's in shock!
JED: Her mum obviously never goes to Erina Fair.
KEERA: Kids from your year have pretty much all moved away from here. 'Cept you. How come you didn't move?
JED: Because.
KEERA: Sue hates it here.

JED: Well, I like it here.

KEERA: Sue never says she's from here. She only ever says 'The Coast' when Sydney people ask, and then they think she's from Terrigal.

JED: Yeah well, I think it's great. Bush, beach ... I can be bodysurfing and twenty minutes later riding a motorbike in the bush. Can't do that in Newtown or Kings Cross, can I?

KEERA: Have you got a motorbike?

JED: [*admitting*] No.

KEERA: Hey ... do you call your sperm-and-egg mum, 'Mum', or your other mum?

> JED *is slightly amused.*

JED: Sperm and what?

KEERA: Sperm and egg. That's how life starts. I read that in a book Mum bought me from a shop near the station. Do you know that shop? It's gone now, it closed down. Hey, has your dad ever sent you like posters or stuff from Hollywood?

> JED *is no longer amused.*

JED: Okay ... just stop talking now.

KEERA: My sister Sue told me your dad was a Hollywood movie star, with an Academy Award and everything, and he met your mum when he was here, ages before he was famous, and they did it, that sperm-and-egg thing, but now she's a lesbian.

JED: [*turning on her*] You know what ... I don't even believe this *is* a naturally forming hole. If you ask me, someone dug it. *Someone* who could get into a lot of trouble.

KEERA: This is because I said that stuff about your dad?

JED: Shut up! Some of us have actual things to do. Jobs. Important things, not basket weaving or storytelling or digging fake holes or whatever retards like you like to do.

> *Pause.*

Sorry.

KEERA: What did you call me? A retard? I'm going to make a complaint. What's the name of your manager? Frank?

JED: I said I'm sorry.

> *Slight pause.*

Look, I do remember Sue and ... Yes ... I still have her pencil case if she wants it back. And yes, my birth mum is Caryl. My other mum is Jane. I call both mums 'Mum', and sometimes I call them Jane and Caryl. And no, I've never had anything sent from ... Hollywood. Ever.

Silence.

I want to keep this job. I'm sorry, okay?

KEERA: I talk too much, everyone says that. I get in trouble all the time.

JED: No, you ... you say what you're thinking. That's a good thing. You tell the truth.

KEERA: We're friends now, aren't we?

Slight pause. JED *nods. She smiles.*

And also ... reckon I can get a selfie with your dad? With him doing rabbit ears behind my head, and me laughing fit to bust, like we know each other really well?

Silence.

JED: [*finally*] What if ... he's not a movie star?

KEERA: What else would he be?

JED: I don't know.

KEERA: He won an Oscar. How can he do that if he's not a movie star?

JED: I don't know.

KEERA: Sue said—

JED: Sue could be wrong, okay? Everyone could be wrong.

KEERA: But your mum, your sperm-and-egg mum ...

JED: No. She never said, she's never said that. Neither of them have ever said that.

Pause.

If he really was my dad, really, why has he never ever tried to contact me, never written or phoned, never sent a birthday card or even acknowledged that he had a kid here ...?

KEERA: Because, he didn't know about you. He left before you were born. Your mum was a single mum and just brought you up the best way she could, and then she met your other mum and they decided to make a new life ... in Wyong ...

JED: That's what you've been told. By people like your sister. It's stuff that kids used to say at school ... rumours.

KEERA: Because it's true. Isn't it?

Silence.

A voice from inside the house.

KEERA'S FATHER: [*offstage*] Keera. What the hell are you doing out there?

KEERA: [*quietly*] I better go. [*Calling back*] Nothing!

JED: You haven't done anything.

KEERA: I never do. Maybe you'll come back? That hole is definitely getting bigger. I promise.

KEERA'S FATHER: [*offstage*] Keera. Don't make me come out there.

KEERA: [*to* JED] If he comes out here, say I've gone to school, okay?

JED: Is that where you're going?

KEERA: Maybe. Maybe I just need to get away from him.

KEERA'S FATHER: [*offstage*] Keera!

JED: [*suddenly*] I'll probably come back.

KEERA: [*hopeful*] Really?

JED: Well, if it *is* a sinkhole, that's pretty serious, ay?

KEERA: That's what I said!

JED: Right, and it could be ...

KEERA'S FATHER: [*offstage, shouting*] Keera! You're meant to be at school!

She runs. JED *watches her go.*

JED: ... dangerous.

SCENE SIX

JANE *stands by Caryl's hospital bed. Looking out the window?*

JANE: I told Jed ... you'll be home soon.

She glances at Caryl. Looks away again.

I don't know how long it's been since I caught the train to Newcastle. Or ... Hamilton, I should say. You get used to the car, don't you?

Pause.

Dad drove trains, but they were freight ... not passenger trains. He told me, a lot of drivers didn't want to do the cities, because, sometimes, people ... you know ... threw themselves under the train. And Dad said ... sometimes ... kids'd put rocks on the lines. Or throw things off rail bridges or at the windows. Little buggers. That's in the seventies and eighties ... We complain about kids today but they were just as bad back then.

Pause.

Big trains, freight trains. Sometimes three engines, one at the back say and two at the front, and in between could be ... sixty trucks or more ... Hard to slow something like that down, let alone stop quickly ...

He came home once and he was pretty shocked because he thought he killed a kid. A boy. Kid'd been fishing with his mates off a bridge. Train takes all that room, see, and he thought maybe, this kid had fallen down under the wheels ... and all that time it takes to stop. They did stop the train and the police were called and they found out the kid had jumped in the river with his mates. I remember Dad telling Mum about it. His hands. Shaking.

He used to sleep during the day—we had no idea when he was working or sleeping, if it was day and we got home from school it was always, 'Shhhh, your father's asleep. Shhhhhhhh.'

Slight pause.

Like, our entire house was a quiet carriage.

Silence. JANE *sits down by the bed. Smoothes a blanket.*

I told Jed ... you'll be home soon. And you will. You will.

SCENE SEVEN

Sound of the train.

PASSENGERS *alight, depart, move seats.*

Soundtrack—snippets of music (grunge or classical), podcasts or recorded conversation.

Nobody makes contact. Nobody speaks out loud.

Everyone is wearing or looking at a device.

Everyone wears earphones.

Some people text.

Some people listen to music or are mid-conversation.

Soundtrack fades into ... sound of the train.

And fades.

SCENE EIGHT

At Frank's office.

JED: That house. With the sinkhole.

FRANK: Purported sinkhole. In fact, don't say the word 'sink'. Or even the word 'hole'. What's another word for 'hole'?

JED: Wyong?

FRANK: No-one likes a smartarse, Jeremy.

JED: Ditch? Hollow? Depression? Pit?

FRANK: Better.

JED: Fine. The house with the unexplained ... basin pit. There's an old guy there.

FRANK: What's your point?

JED: He's weird. That's my point. Is there something I'm meant to know? About his daughter?

FRANK: Daughter? She's gone to Sydney, hasn't she?

JED: The younger one. Still at school.

FRANK: That's right. Forgot he had two girls. The young one's two sandwiches short of a picnic, if I remember. Some sort of accident when she was a baby. Bloke's alright. Rooster, we call him. Harmless.

JED: Harmless? What about his daughter? She's scared of him.

FRANK: Everyone's scared of their dad sometimes. Though I was more scared of my mum. She used to come at me with the jug cord.

JED: Yeah, well things have changed since your days, Frank. We don't stick kids up chimneys anymore either.

FRANK: Steady on. Rooster's alright. He's just a ... lost soul.

JED: Well, he's a pretty angry lost soul.

FRANK: You call this place a hole, Jeremy? What this place is ... is a town full of lost souls. Start with the kids, they got nothing to do, nothing they want to do, they may as well fall through one of your sinkholes to the other side of the world. They reckon they'd rather be on the dole here than in Sydney. The dollar goes further here, and I'm not talking about groceries. Understand me?

Someone like you, Jeremy, you got yourself a bit of a spark. Don't screw that up. Don't fall in the shit like these others around here. All these lost souls, they had some spark in them, once. Even Rooster. But one falls down the shit and drags in the next one and the next. And all those little sparks go out. And this place gets that bit darker. Do you know what I'm saying here?

Pause.

JED: Don't fall in shit?

FRANK: That'll do. Keep away from Rooster's place, alright? You don't need to be there. We got plenty of other jobs.

He hands JED *a piece of paper.*

There you go. Something a bit easier.

JED: I don't want something a bit easier. I want to make sure Keera's okay.

FRANK: Who's Keera?

Beat.

JED: No-one.

JED *takes the paper and goes.* FRANK *calls after him.*

FRANK: I mean it, Jeremy. You're still on probation. Keep away from there.

SCENE NINE

JED *is setting up a ring of flags around the sinkhole and making notes as* KEERA *watches him. If we can see the hole we will note that it is bigger.*

KEERA: Mississippi. An entire car park, gone. People were sitting in a restaurant eating their dinner. And they heard a noise and they looked up and saw, through the windows, their cars just … dropping, in front of them. They've got drone footage of the hole and it's like massive.

Beat.

Are you sure you're meant to put that stuff around a sinkhole? Little flags?

JED: It's not 'little flags'. It's bunting. It's Official Sinkhole Bunting. Council Approved.

KEERA: I didn't know they used that.

JED: Of course you didn't. Who's the Council Sinkhole Inspector here?

KEERA: You.

JED: That's right. I showed you my certificate, right?

> JED *looks at her briefly and goes back to putting things around the hole.*

KEERA: And in China. Just in the middle of a street in the city. You see this woman just walking along and suddenly this hole opens in the footpath and she just drops through. Just like that.

JED: What sort of restaurant?

KEERA: What?

JED: Where all the cars fell into the hole. What sort of restaurant?

KEERA: [*thinking*] Mexican? Not sure. I'll have to google.

> JED *nods. He pulls out some stuffed toys and starts to place them around the hole.*

Do you need those?

JED: Yes. Obviously, otherwise I wouldn't do it. And before you ask, yes, one has to be a penguin.

> *He starts blowing up a few balloons and tying them to the bunting as he talks.*

How's it going with your dad?

KEERA: Are you worried he'll yell at me again? He's not here.

JED: [*careful*] Does he … yell at you a lot?

KEERA: I get in trouble. I don't mean to.

JED: You know your sister, who went to Sydney …

KEERA: Of course. Sue. I miss her.

JED: Do you ever go see her? Maybe, spend time with her?

> JED *is trying to delicately plant this idea …*

KEERA: I would love to go and see her. And she would love to see me. I talk to her on the phone and she's always saying I should visit her. She said we could go to Luna Park.

JED: That's great. So ... she could come and get you. You could leave here and stay with her?

KEERA: Yes!

Slight pause.

I've never seen balloons used for sinkholes on the internet.

JED: We're trialling some things. And, um, you're sure no-one's been doing any ... extracurricular digging.

KEERA: Of course not.

JED: Good. Because that would be illegal and probably a punishable offence. Don't touch this. Don't go off anywhere, okay? Except school. Go to school. I'll see you tomorrow.

KEERA: Promise?

JED: 'Course. I'm the Official Sinkhole Inspector. It's my job.

Sound of a train passing in the background.

SCENE TEN

JED *and* JANE *at home.* JED *is eating dinner.*

JANE: Caryl loved those pictures.

JED: What pictures?

JANE: The ones I took on your first day of work. You looked so good.

JED: You didn't cry?

JANE: A tiny bit. A smidge.

JED: And when's she coming home?

Tiny pause.

JANE: Very soon. A couple of days. I'd say.

JED: The weekend? Did she say the weekend?

Beat.

JANE: She asked about your work. What sort of things you do. Who you work with. I don't really know ... what *do* you do?

JED: Filing things mostly. Computer stuff.

JANE: Well, you're good at that.

JED: Spreadsheets.

JANE: Spreadsheets! Great. I hope everyone's being nice to you. No left-handed spanners ... or long stands?

JED: There's this old guy Frank, he got me a beauty.

JANE: Oh, Frank. I know Frank. Why'd they put you with *him*?

JED: Um. Spreadsheet. He needed a hand.

JANE: He's a funny stick.

JED: That's one way of describing him. Cranky old bastard's another.

JANE: He's not old! He's Caryl's age! You wouldn't think that to look at him, but he was in her year at school.

Slight pause.

We're really proud of you. Mum and I. You know that, right?

JED: Don't know why. Haven't done anything.

JANE: This past year has been pretty hard.

JED: Pretty boring, you mean.

JANE: At one stage we thought we were going to lose you to the Land of Couch Potato …

JED: The what?

JANE: [*laughing*] Nothing. I just mean … there's a lot of kids round here who finish school—or don't finish school—and they live their life just lying about on their couch, or drinking or getting stoned. And … that's not you. It's … not in your genes. You've got a spark.

JED: A spark?

JANE: You used to draw a lot when you were at high school. Maybe you could think about applying to one of the art schools. In Sydney or Melbourne …

JED: There's no way I'd be good enough.

JANE: Well, you won't know unless you try, will you? I'm going back to the hospital tomorrow. Do you want to come?

JED: I thought she said she was back on the weekend.

JANE: Basically. Yes.

JED: So … I've got work.

JANE: I know.

JED: So what about that business with me having a spark and not being a couch potato or getting drunk or stoned?

JANE: It's just one day …

JED: It's a slippery slope, Jane. One day I don't go to work, next day I'm spewing in a gutter somewhere.

JANE: You could ask someone—

JED: Someone like Frank? Doubt it …

JANE: I've got a friend at council, Gina, she could have a word.

JED: No, no, don't do that …

JANE: She knows things have been hard for you …

JED: Why does she know that? Did she say that to you?

JANE: She's being nice.

JED: Real nice. Talking behind my back?

JANE: It's not that. She remembers you as a kid. She actually, she remembered this funny rumour about you, do you remember when kids at your school used to think you were like some secret Aussie Love Child of … what's that movie star's name?

JED *stops eating.*

Crazy. The rumours that float around this town, honestly!

She laughs.

Remember the rumour, when everyone thought that soccer star was going to play with the Mariners here? For some reason everyone just went nuts about it. I don't even like sports much, but I kind of got into it because he was married to one of the Spice Girls and so that was, you know, sort of thrilling that maybe one of the Spice Girls would visit Wyong, probably not stay over but, you know, might drive through, visit the Reptile Park, that sort of thing. Jed?

She looks around. He's gone.

Little bugger.

She picks up the plates.

Then realises.

Got it!

Beat.

David Beckham.

SCENE ELEVEN

Sound of a train …

RAILWAY ANNOUNCER: Passengers are reminded that there is no smoking on the train. Next station is Fassifern. Fassifern next stop.

JED *is fiddling with an iPod and headphones. Pissed off.*

JED: On the train.

Trying to cool down.

Calm carriage. Quiet carriage. Headphones tied in a knot. Gah!

ACTOR 2: Do you mind turning that music down?

JED: [*trying to keep his cool*] Calm carriage.

ACTOR 3: Do you mind if I take this seat?

JED: Quiet carriage!

ACTOR 4: Do you mind not staring at me, mate?

Slight pause. JED *turns away, boiling.*

ACTOR 2: Not talking.

ACTOR 3: Not laughing.

ACTOR 4: Not breathing.

RAILWAY ANNOUNCER: Passengers are reminded that there is no smoking anywhere on the train.

From left: Tallulah Cobbin, Jackson Vaughan as Jed, Angie Diaz and Christopher Saunders in Tantrum Youth Arts' 2016 production.
(Photo: Claire Albrecht)

JED: [*at near breaking point*] Don't touch people.

    Don't talk to people.

    Don't make eye contact.

    Blokes on ice.

    Chicks with mates who take offence. Want someone to punch.

    Old men going off their nut at young Asian women. Speak English!

    Gangs of white boys screaming abuse at brown schoolkids.

    Don't stop. Don't help. Don't save.

ACTOR 4: Ch *ch*, ch *ch*

    ch *ch*, ch *ch* ...

ACTOR 2: Look at your phone.

ACTOR 4: Look out the window.

ACTOR 3: Look the other way.

    JED *takes a deep breath.*

JED: Through the window. Looks grey. Dark clouds approaching.

ACTOR 4: Whistle.

RAILWAY ANNOUNCER: Doors closing please, stand clear.

ACTOR 4: Ch *ch*, ch *ch*

    ch *ch*, ch *ch* ...

    Beat.

KEERA: Jed!

    JED *is startled.*

JED: Keera.

KEERA: Are you going somewhere?

JED: No. Needed to get out. Clear my head.

KEERA: What's wrong with your head?

JED: Nothing. Something Jane was saying.

KEERA: About your dad?

JED: No ... yes. No!

KEERA: I think I can help you!

JED: I said no, Keera!

KEERA: Remember that movie: *How To Lose A Guy In 10 Days*?

JED: He's not my dad! It's just a stupid rumour. Leave it.

KEERA: But I'm talking about finding your *real* dad.

JED: What *real* dad?

KEERA: I'm trying to tell you. In the movie. It's when Ben spots Andie. And he sees her face and it's like he knows straight away … she's the one. They click. So what if your real dad's some ordinary guy, what if your mum met him on the train?

JED: Twenty years ago?

KEERA: So? People catch the train for years. What if … you see his face? Now. And something clicks.

JED: And I think he's the one? You want me to base this on a romantic comedy. That's very scientific.

KEERA: It's not meant to be science. It's emotion. First impressions. Look … that guy … just think … 'Dad?'

> *She points.* JED *looks.*

Well? Feel anything?

JED: Man, sensible orange parka. Cropped hair. Bad skin.

KEERA: Wouldn't be the sensible parka type. Surely. Would he?

JED: Don't know. Hope not.

> *She points out someone else.*

KEERA: That one?

JED: Brown hair. Beaky nose. Laptop-addicted. Looks at me, and …

KEERA: And?

ACTOR 4: [*to them*] This is the quiet carriage. Can you keep your voices down?

JED: [*to* KEERA] No.

> *She points at another.*

KEERA: That one? First impressions?

JED: Bald. Flowing beard. Reading a book on … *Rainbow Tantra and Post 9/11 Kundalini.* No thanks.

KEERA: Come on. Keep looking.

JED: This is crazy.

ACTOR 3: Train trundles past the high school.

JED: 'Starter kits'! 'Home brew'!

ACTOR 3: Stop to let the fast trains through.

KEERA: 'Clearance sale now on!' 'Selected cocktail flavourings!'

ACTOR 4: Small rain
spatters window.

ACTOR 3: Faster train …
ACTOR 4: better train …
ACTOR 3: bangs past.

> *Pause.*

JED: It's not as if I thought I'd get some invite to Hollywood …
ACTOR 4: Grey stone seats,
ACTOR 3: palm trees,
ACTOR 4: pizza,
JED: Run up a red carpet with my father, I never thought that.
ACTOR 3: terracotta,
  brick fragments,
  bleak stones,
ACTOR 4: water,
  seeps down rocky faces,
  grey concrete walls,
JED: It's not like I expected him to call me 'son' …
ACTOR 3: hidden garden,
ACTOR 4: pebble paths,
KEERA: forty-four-gallon drums,
JED: But having someone famous for a dad, even if I didn't actually have
  him …
ACTOR 3: car yards, painted skate ramp,
JED: I had the spark. Because of him. And now, it's gone … and I'm
  falling.
KEERA: wet pools in footy fields,
  mud puddling,
ACTOR 3: rain sloshing against the window,
KEERA: until finally,
ACTOR 4: bright gleam on wet surface.
  Gum leaves and tin roofs.
  Rain stops.

> *Pause.*

KEERA: Jed, your mum. Caryl. She's not coming home from hospital, is
  she?

> *Short pause.*

JED: Jane said. She's having more tests.

> *Pause.*

KEERA: Sometimes, people do come back. Even from a sinkhole. That girl in China who fell through the footpath. Someone went in and got her. And she was alive.

> *Beat.*

JED: Are you sure that's not just some movie you saw?

> *Silence.* JED *turns away. Angry.*

RAILWAY ANNOUNCER: Next stop is Fassifern. Fassifern next stop.

KEERA: We should go to Fassifern!

JED: We should get back. You've got homework.

KEERA: You sound like my dad.

> *A moment.*

JED: I'm not your dad. I'm not your brother or one of your mates from school. Do what you want. I don't care.

> *He turns away.*

KEERA: You're still coming tomorrow, aren't you?

JED: I don't reckon I will.

KEERA: Please.

JED: No.

KEERA: But you said … you're the Sinkhole Inspector.

> *Pause.*

Aren't you?

POLICE OFFICER: Morning all, check your tickets please.

KEERA: [*alarmed*] Check-your-tickets police. [*Hissing*] Jed …

POLICE OFFICER: Tickets please? Thank you.

KEERA: We have to get off. Jed!

RAILWAY ANNOUNCER: Fassifern. This stop.

ACTOR 4: Fassifern. Where old ladies depart.

ACTOR 3: Grey hair, sturdy jackets. Bags printed 'Art Gallery of NSW'.

OLD LADY 1: I loved the Monet.

OLD LADY 2: Too much modern for me.

POLICE OFFICER: [*seeing* JED *and* KEERA] You two … tickets?

KEERA: Move it! Jed!

Push him along,
stand by doors,
ready to jump and …

> *She jumps onto the platform. Laughing.*

Off!
Push through, spill onto the platform.
Safe.

> *Beat.*

Jed?

> *She looks back. He's still in the doorway.*

JED: 'Bye, Keera.
RAILWAY ANNOUNCER: Doors closing. Please stand clear.

> *Doors close.* JED *turns away.*

KEERA: [*alarmed*] Jed!

> *She bangs on the door.*

> *Sound of the train passing. Driver sounds the horn.*

SCENE TWELVE

KEERA *is by the sinkhole. She has a shovel. She digs out some dirt. Puts the shovel down. Peers into the hole.*

KEERA: What happened was … the first brother had gone to bed and the second brother was in the toilet or something and suddenly there was a noise like a train smashed through a wall. *Wham!*
The second brother could hear the first brother screaming out his name. So he ran into the first brother's bedroom and there was just … nothing.
Where his bed had been was a huge hole and it was getting bigger. The floor was crumbling down into it and all the clothes and books and stuff round the edges of the room were dropping into this gaping huge hole and the first brother … was gone.
The second brother tried to pull him out, he tried to jump in and pull him right out, but it didn't work, he couldn't see him, he couldn't hear him.
He was gone.

I wonder about that first brother. Like, was he asleep or jumping on the bed, maybe he did one of those big flying leaps from across the room just like he did every night, but this night when he landed, *boom*, that was it, he was gone.

You see the second brother, crying, and you wonder if he'll ever survive that grief. It's like a gap, a part of him missing, left by someone who just … disappears.

SCENE THIRTEEN

Sound of the train.

Soundtrack—snippets of music (grunge or classical), podcasts or recorded conversation.

PASSENGERS *milling.*

Nobody makes contact. Nobody speaks out loud.

Everyone is wearing or looking at a device.

Everyone wears earphones.

Some people text.

Some people listen to music or are mid-conversation.

Soundtrack fades into …

Sound of the train.

SCENE FOURTEEN

Later.

JANE *is sitting, waiting for* JED. *She has opened the violin case and is looking at the violin. She runs the bow over the strings, making a horrible noise.* JED *enters. He goes to walk past her.*

JANE: [*putting down the violin*] Where have you been?
JED: Work.

> JANE *nods. She's angry but trying to keep a lid on it.*

JANE: Work? More spreadsheets?
JED: That's right.
JANE: That's bullshit.
JED: What's up with you?

JANE: Do you know a girl called Keera?

JED: Why?

JANE: Because she's gone.

JED: What do you mean 'gone'.

JANE: I mean … she ran away. She left a note saying she was going to Sydney. Apparently you might know something about it.

JED: Why would I know?

JANE: Because according to Keera's father, you were mentioned in her note. Have you got something to do with it?

JED: Keera's father should be the first suspect. I haven't done anything.

JANE: You've been in their yard, you bring stuff for her, toys and flags and all sorts of crap. He thinks you've had some sort of relationship with her.

JED: Relationship? That's disgusting. She's like a kid. She's just a friend. Not even that, I met her because of my job.

JANE: Your job! Yes, let's talk about 'your job'. Because according to Gina, you haven't been anywhere near 'your job' for the past few days.

JED: Yes I have.

JANE: No you haven't. Which is weird when you consider … you started the day before you were meant to …

JED: Okay, so Frank dobbed me in …?

JANE: Actually, Frank said you were bright, intelligent and chock-full of initiative. He also said you were out assessing something called 'basin pits' at a number of houses, including Keera's. This turned out to be completely false, Gina rang every house to find out if you or Keera had been there.

JED: Why would she do that?

JANE: Because I asked her to, alright, Jed? That's how I know you've been lying. And now this girl is gone …

JED: Because her father's a psycho.

JANE: His daughter has an intellectual disability. He's worried that she'll be in danger. He is not a psycho. He is a worried and concerned parent. Just like I am a worried and concerned parent …

JED: You don't listen to me, you never listen to what I'm saying. Forget it, I'm going.

He starts to walk out. She might even grab him. Both are furious.

JANE: Don't you dare walk out, we are having a conversation. You want to be treated like an adult, stop acting like a child.

JED: Stop treating me like a child, then.

JANE: Then stop lying to me!

JED: [*stopping, cracking it*] I am not the liar! You. And Caryl. You both lied to me. If I'm not a kid, then tell me the truth about my father.

JANE: You don't have a father! You have two mothers!

JED: I know that! But once upon a time someone gave Caryl some sperm and it wasn't you.

> *Both, horrified.*

JANE: You little … shit!

JED: I'm sorry!

JANE: No you're not. You want the truth? Fine.

> *They stare at each other, angry.*

> *Sound of trains.*

SCENE FIFTEEN

On the train.

RAILWAY ANNOUNCER: Next stop. Wyong. Followed by Warnervale, Wyee. Passengers disembarking at Warnervale and Wyee, please do so from the rear four cars due to short platforms.

ACTOR 4: Road runs beside us.

JED: Watching. Looking at faces. Run through every carriage. Images flash past me.

ACTOR 4: 'Pride Mowers', grey hatchback, green trees.

RAILWAY ANNOUNCER: Wyong.

JED: Stand up now. Watch everyone who gets off.

ACTOR 3: Watch … Small kid in grey shorts followed by tired-looking woman in yellow coat.

ACTOR 4: Watch … Teenagers. Trackpants. Hoodie. One with a deck under his arm.

JED: Watch … Two chicks, skinny, pale. Nose-ring.

PISSED-OFF BLOKE: Getting off, mate, or just standing in the way?

JED: Sorry, mate, just …

> JED *gets out of the way.* KEERA *appears.*

PISSED-OFF BLOKE: [*to* KEERA] Move it, love, this is my stop.

KEERA: Whoopsie! Sorry.

JED: Keera!

ACTOR 4: Watch him go. Pissed-off bloke in ugly beanie.

JED: Everyone's looking for you. Where the hell have you been?

RAILWAY ANNOUNCER: Doors closing, please stand clear.

KEERA: Ooh, he just made it. That shitty guy who pushed past!

ACTOR 4: Whistle blows.

KEERA: I think he gave us the daggers, from the platform.

> *She gives him the finger.*

JED: Don't do that, Keera.

KEERA: [*pointing out a man*] Hey! See that one? Through the window. Grown man on a swing. Is that your real dad? Did he like swings?

JED: Keera. You've been gone since yesterday. You need to go home.

KEERA: [*still looking at the man*] Nah ... don't like his jumper. Find someone else.

ACTOR 4: Large houses. Suburban houses.

ACTOR 3: Chook runs and swimming pools.

ACTOR 4: And a small blue trailer.

RAILWAY ANNOUNCER: Warnervale. Stop.

JED: Keera. People are worried about you. You've been gone since yesterday.

KEERA: So? Let's get off and have a coffee at Warnies.

JED: Let's *not* have a coffee at Warnies. Keera, stop it! What are you doing?

KEERA: We could have a tea?

> *Beep beep beep.*

RAILWAY ANNOUNCER: Doors closing. Please stand clear.

> *Slight pause.*

KEERA: I just ... wanted to go to Sue's.

JED: So what, you just took off. Without telling anyone?

KEERA: I caught the train to Sydney. I rang Sue when I got to Central but she said ... she said ...

> *Beat.*

She told me she was too busy and I had to get back on the train.

JED: What?

KEERA: So I did get back on the train. And then I went all the way to Hamilton. And then I stayed on the train and went all the way back to Sydney. And I did that all night. And people sleep on the train. Sometimes they sleep on the floor so no-one can see them.

JED: Did you tell her about your father?

KEERA: What about him?

JED: That ... he yells at you.

KEERA: She knows that. He used to yell at her.

JED: That you're scared of him.

KEERA: But. I'm *not* scared of him. Did you think I was?

> *Pause.*

He's okay, my dad. He's just ... strict.

JED: Strict?

KEERA: Since my mum left. And now Sue's gone, even though she comes back at Christmas. He probably freaked out when he saw I was gone too.

JED: Yeah, he freaked out alright. Then he freaked out Frank. And then Jane. I'm in the shit now. Probably lost my job.

KEERA: You still like me though, don't you, Jed? We're still friends.

> *Pause. He turns away.*

JED: Staring through the window,
see
my face in the glass staring back.

KEERA: Jed?

JED: Look at my face. See Mum.
The rest of me must be ... him.

KEERA: Trains are like the best fun. You wanna get off at Cardiff? Catch another one back?

JED: No.

KEERA: Or stay on till Hamilton? Jed? We can play 'Who's Your Dad?' all the way there.

JED: We're not playing anything, Keera, okay?

KEERA: What about that man over there?

JED: No.

KEERA: He still could be a movie star.

JED: He's not a movie star. Would you stop that? He's just …

> *Pause.*

> [*Finally*] Some guy. Some random guy who picked up Caryl at the RSL club. Twenty years ago. She only saw him that night and she was too drunk to remember his name. Jane found her in the car park and got her home. That's how Jane and Caryl met. Romantic, eh?

> Where did that tall guy in the suit get off? What about that man with the bicycle? Briefcase guy from Strathfield? The man in the pink T-shirt who asked how far to Newcastle? And the one reading the paper? And the one eating a KitKat?

> Who's my dad? Just some guy, Keera.

> None of them were him. And any one of them could be him.

RAILWAY ANNOUNCER: A reminder that there are three quiet carriages on this train. They are the first, last and central carriages. Passengers are asked to refrain from loud conversations, playing music or using your mobile phones in these carriages.

JED: I'm just ordinary, Keera. Ordinary. I'm just like anyone else, made up from an ordinary egg and a very ordinary sperm. I'm sorry.

> *Beat.*

> I'm not playing anymore.

> *Silence.* KEERA *turns away.*

RAILWAY ANNOUNCER: Next stop Fassifern. Fassifern next stop.

> *Silence.*

JED: Are you alright?

> *Pause.*

KEERA: I want to go home.

> *Sound of the train …*

SCENE SIXTEEN

Sound of the train continues.

Soundtrack/music.

PASSENGERS *move around the carriage. Sit.*

Soundtrack fades.

Find JED *amidst the train.*

Find JANE.

A moment. JANE *smiles at him, just.*

JED: Jane …

JANE: Thought you might be on a train.

JED: You're lucky. You could have been looking on trains for a week.

JANE: Yeah, well. I would have done it. I would have.

    Pause.

JED: Caryl told me it was just tests and so did you? But it's not, is it? It's more than that.

JANE: She's having treatment, yes.

JED: Cancer.

JANE: Yes. It's cancer.

JED: So … Caryl isn't coming back soon.

    Pause.

JANE: No.

JED: Why didn't you tell me?

JANE: Because you had a new job.

Because we didn't want you to be hurt.

Because you've had a bad year.

Because you're our son.

And because …

    Pause.

JED: So this means … Caryl's going to—

    JANE *stops him.*

JANE: Please.

Don't. Don't say the words.

JED: It's alright. You can tell me. You don't need to hide it. I'm not a kid, Jane.

JANE: I know.

God, I know.

It's not for you. It's for me.

Do you understand?
I can't hear those words out loud.

She's crying.

She starts to turn from him. JED *grabs her into a hug.*

ACTOR 4: Excuse me?

JED *and* JANE *look around.*

This is a *quiet* carriage.

SCENE SEVENTEEN

Later.

JED *stands on the bridge at Wyong station, looking down on the tracks.*
FRANK *walks up beside him. Looks down over the bridge.*
Sound of the trains.

FRANK: Love watching the trains from up here. Don't you?

Silence. He looks at JED.

You alright, mate?

JED: What are you doing here, Frank?

FRANK: It's just. You've been standing here a while. [*Awkwardly*] R U
OK? They tell you to ask that, you know. If you see someone who
looks a bit dodgy.

Pause.

JED: Are you watching me? You think I look dodgy.

FRANK: It's just, you know, blokes on train bridges, you get a bit worried,
don't you? Blokes on any sort of bridge really.

JED *looks at him.*

JED: What do you mean, you've seen me standing here for a while? Are
you following me?

FRANK: No.

Slight pause.

There's that bookshop, near the station, educational—

JED: Bullshit. It's closed. Are you some kind of pervert, Frank? I do
aikido, just so you know. Touch me: I flip you straight over the edge.

FRANK: No need for that.

JED: Well, there is if you are actually some kind of pervert, there's plenty of need.

FRANK: Okay. Sorry. Just haven't seen you for a bit. Didn't know what you were up to.

JED: Stuff been going on. Lot to think about. I got the sack.

FRANK: Yeah, well. I've been sacked from plenty of jobs. I know a coupla blokes here at the station if you're looking for something.

JED: Thinking about something else. Applying to art school.

FRANK: Yeah, good.

JED: Scared but.

FRANK: What? Of a bunch of paintbrush-wielding hipsters? Come off it. You're a Coastie.

JED: What happens if I stuff that up? And then I have to come back here? Everyone knows. Massive fail. Shame.

FRANK: Nah. No shame. Surprised you haven't gone already.

JED: Mum's sick.

Slight pause.

FRANK: Sorry.

JED: She was meant to come home after having some tests, but they kept her at the hospital. She's having an operation but … they said … she might not survive it. You wouldn't think something could happen so fast. It's like she's just … crumbling.

FRANK: Sometimes … it is fast.

JED: Sometimes it feels like I've got this hole here in my gut, getting bigger and bigger every day.

FRANK: You'll be alright …

JED *looks at him.*

I'm not saying she'll get better, nothing like that. Just that, I can tell, you'll get through this. You got a spark in you.

JED: Thanks.

FRANK: Can … I could call someone for you? You got a dad?

JED: No. Don't have a dad. I've got Jane. She's my … other mum. She's pretty good.

FRANK: Two mums?

JED: Yeah.

Silence.

RAILWAY ANNOUNCER: The train arriving at Platform One goes to Central. First stop Tuggerah. Then Gosford. Then Woy Woy. Hornsby. Eastwood. Epping. Strathfield. And Central.

Silence.

FRANK: That's mine. Big smoke. Night out.

JED: Frank … how come *you* never left Wyong?

FRANK: Like it here. Like it a lot. You got the bush and the beach. Twenty minutes from one to the other.

JED: That's what I say.

RAILWAY ANNOUNCER: The train arriving at Platform Two goes to Newcastle. First stop Morisset. Then Fassifern. Cardiff. Broadmeadow. Hamilton. Change at Hamilton for bus to Newcastle.

JED: That's mine.

FRANK: Yeah. Been here all my life.

He gestures at the train approaching.

Better head down there … and … sorry about Caryl.

He puts out his hand for JED *to shake.*

A moment.

They shake and then head to opposite sides of the bridge.

Sound of a train passing.

SCENE EIGHTEEN

Sound of a violin playing Vivaldi's 'Summer'.

As it plays, we see Keera's moonlit front yard.

Find KEERA *finishing filling in the hole. She gathers up the bunting and balloons.*

Finally, she sits by the hole. Hugs the penguin. Looks up at the sky.

In a separate light FRANK *appears.*

FRANK: They say it's water that causes a sinkhole, eats away, slowly underground. Acidic rainwater seeping down, through surface dirt, eroding bedrock. Chances of that happening around here though … pfft.

In a separate light, JED *appears at one side of the stage.*

JANE *appears at the other. Sees* JED, *smiles.*

JED: Mum?

JANE: She's awake. You can see her.

JANE *gestures behind her, towards the room.* JED *goes to walk past her, then stops.*

JED: Mum.

He reaches to JANE *and she takes his hand.*

They walk in together.

Vivaldi's 'Summer' finishes.

THE END

ALSO AVAILABLE FROM CURRENCY PRESS

Jasper Jones
Based on the book by Craig Silvey and
adapted for the stage by Kate Mulvany

It's summer 1965 in a small, hot town in Western Australia. Overseas,
war is raging in Vietnam, Civil Rights marches are on the streets,
and women's liberation is stirring – but at home in Corrigan Charlie
Bucktin dreams of writing the Great Australian Novel. Charlie's
14 and smart. But when 16-year-old, constantly-in-trouble Jasper
Jones appears at his window one night, Charlie's out of his depth.
Jasper has stumbled upon a terrible crime in the scrub nearby,
and he knows he's the first suspect – that goes with the colour
of his skin. He needs every ounce of Charlie's bookish brain to
help solve this awful mystery before the town turns on Jasper.

Kate Mulvany's adaptation of Craig Silvey's award-winning novel is wise
and beautiful – it features a cast of finely drawn teenagers and grown-
ups, all searching for their own kind of truth. A coming-of-age story,
Jasper Jones interweaves the lives of complex individuals all struggling to
find happiness among the buried secrets of a small rural community.

'Whether you know the book or not, this piercing adaptation is
very much worth seeing for the way it depicts – and shows ways
across – some of the deep and enduring divides in our society.'
Jason Blake, *Sydney Morning Herald*

ISBN 978 1 76062 004 2

Michael Swordfish
Lachlan Philpott

'You read about those kids who know they don't belong. They are in some kind of prison until they turn 18, stuck in the backseat of the car between two kids who do belong.'

What would happen if someone you knew disappeared? How would you react? How would your school react? An assembly called, a footy game postponed, a class interrupted. But who is Michael Swordfish? And who knows where he's gone?

For two years award-winning playwright Lachlan Philpott collaborated with students from Newington College, Sydney, to bring their voices and worlds to life. *Michael Swordfish* is the exciting product of this collaboration: a play that traverses the tumultuous landscape of the teenage experience with a sober truth and darkly comic voice.

Winner of the AWGIE Award for Youth and Community Theatre (2017).

ISBN 978 1 76062 083 7

Parasites
Ninna Tersman

I dream about flying
I'm flying while
The world under me is—
On fire

Two teenagers fleeing unthinkable dangers find solace in each
other amidst the unrelentingly damaging confines of an asylum
seeker processing centre. Their new 'home' offers a kind of safety,
but very little in the way of humanity, and less kindness.

Ninna Tersman's writing is poetic, spare, and deeply human. She
plays with theatrical form in many ways. The two actors in *Parasites*
play the teenagers and a number of adults who impact their lives.

This is the tender story of young people in a desperate
situation, yearning for hope and home.

ISBN 978 1 76062 053 0

The Violent Outburst That Drew Me To You
Finegan Kruckemeyer

Sixteen-year-old Connor is angry. He doesn't know why, and he doesn't know where to direct it. People and things he once liked annoy him. His parents, his best friend, his once-cool uncle now officially suck. Then, the outburst. Connor is dropped in a forest for a week by himself to calm down. But his anger has travelled with him.

Then a girl called Lotte walks into the woods. And she is angry too...

From Inaugural Sidney Myer Creative Fellowship recipient Finegan Kruckemeyer comes this smart, sweet and fiery tale about two offbeat kids who, at war with the world, find a moment's peace with each other. It's a reminder of the impatient impulse in all of us to kick and scream at the universe, and the equally impatient impulse to lie in a forest glade and plan for the future.

'Funny without being patronising, and serious without seeming earnest... *The Violent Outburst That Drew Me To You* develops a hallucinatory quality which feels just right.'
Jason Blake, *Sydney Morning Herald*

ISBN 978 1 92500 532 5

Brisbane
Matthew Ryan

'The air is thick and wet and the sun burns your skin like it hates your guts ... It's 1942 and I'm fourteen, which means I face two obstacles on a daily basis. One: Entire countries that want to kill me. And two: The Cricket Boys on Mulvany Street.'

Danny Fisher is coming of age at a time when Brisbane faces the threat of extinction. When his beloved brother Frank is killed in the bombing of Darwin, Danny's family is ripped apart. Ignored by grieving parents, the awkward Danny is left to fend for himself, and to try to fill the shoes left behind. Thrust headlong into the threat of war and the hope of love, Danny, like his city, is growing up fast. Aided by his potty-mouthed best-friend Patty, Danny meets an American serviceman identical to Danny's lost brother. But when the American begins teaching him how to fly, Danny comes up with a dangerous plan to prove his own worth.

Ripe with understated larrikinism and emotional resonance, *Brisbane* is a celebration of a city and a childhood – and a requiem for all that was lost.

'Ryan's script is rich, textured and very funny at times.
This is a winner. And it's our story.' *The Courier Mail*

'Brisbane is a testament to just how vital and engaging even historical theatre can be ... A surprisingly riveting, insightful and accessible self-portrait of some of the city's most turbulent days.'
The Creative Issue

ISBN 978 1 92500 560 8

A Town Named War Boy
Ross Mueller

'We hit Cairo like a train!... Every dirty little alley, every dusty
back room bar. The pyramids are marvellous, but I could spend the
rest of my days quite happily in the arms of your temptation.'

Inspired by The State Library of New South Wales' jaw-dropping
collection of World War I diaries and letters, *A Town Named War Boy*
explores both the events of war and the impact it has upon soldiers
and their families. Written with insight, humour and sensitivity,
Ross Mueller's moving play brings the ANZAC legend to life.

ISBN 978 1 92500 539 4

The Incredible Here and Now
Felicity Castagna

Charcoal chicken, a white Pontiac Trans Am, the Council pool, Michael is living in the shadow of his older brother Dom. The biggest guy in the school. Best car in the West. The guy who just can't help but grab everyone's attention. The guy with the girlfriend with the huge-arse hair.

When he is gone Michael roams the streets, navigating life, friendship, love and family. *The Incredible Here and Now* is a poignant rollercoaster ride celebrating life, first love, family and new beginnings, traversing the streets of Western Sydney.

Adapted for the stage by international award-winning local author and playwright Felicity Castagna.

ISBN 978 1 76062 133 9

Checklist for an Armed Robber
Vanessa Bates

On 23 October 2002, Chechen rebels stormed a theatre in Moscow, holding hundreds of theatre-goers hostage. Three days later, in Newcastle, Australia, a young man staged an armed robbery in a bookshop. *Checklist for an Armed Robber* picks up the threads of these two real life evens and weaves them together in an attempt to better examine the complex patterns of violence, courage and empathy. This AWGIE-winning play from Vanessa Bates observes with sensitivity and humour the perspective from both ends of the gun.

ISBN 978 0 86819 863 7

Contemporary Australian Monologues

Monologues are a crucial element of theatre, for actors and students alike. From high school study to professional auditions and performances, the monologue exposes the heart of a play and the capacities of the performer.

The monologue should be relevant to the performer, and a revelation to the audience. These new collections each bring together 30 monologues from contemporary Australian plays. These voices—from ages 14 to 84, from the 1880s to the near future—showcase the best of our national writing for the stage.

Featuring monologues from:
Donna Abela • Jada Alberts • Angela Betzien • Jane Bodie • Andrew Bovell • Kit Brookman • Nicholas Brown & Sam McCool • Melissa Bubnic • Mary Anne Butler • Justine Campbell & Sarah Hamilton • Stephen Carleton • Katherine Thomson, Angela Chaplin & Kavisha Mazzella • Elizabeth Coleman • Patricia Cornelius • Brendan Cowell • Wesley Enoch • Eamon Flack • Richard Frankland • Michael Gow • Jane Montgomery Griffiths • R. Johns • Rashma N. Kalsie • Daniel Keene • Finegan Kruckemeyer • Suzie Miller • Ross Mueller • Luke Mullins & Lachlan Philpott • Kate Mulvany & Craig Silvey • Tommy Murphy & Timothy Conigrave • Joanna Murray-Smith • Terence O'Connell • Debra Oswald • Lachlan Philpott • Leah Purcell • Melissa Reeves • Caroline Reid • Damien Ryan • Matthew Ryan • Samah Sabawi • Stephen Sewell • Ninna Tersman • Katherine Thomson • Christos Tsiolkas • Alana Valentine • Matthew Whittet

For women: ISBN 978 1 76062 176 6
For men: ISBN 978 1 76062 177 3